FOR JOANNA
whose caring and sharing
has made this book possible

·J·U·S·T·
·F·O·R·

you

MARION STROUD

A LION BOOK
Tring · Belleville · Sydney

Copyright © 1986 Lion Publishing

Published by
Lion Publishing plc
Icknield Way, Tring, Herts, England
ISBN 0 85648 910 7
Albatross Books
PO Box 320, Sutherland, NSW 2232, Australia
ISBN 0 86760 639 8

First edition 1986

Acknowledgments
The following items appear by kind permission
of the copyright holders:
Tim Hansel quotation, p.46, reprinted with permission from *When I Relax
I Feel Guilty*, ©1979 David C. Cook Publishing Co., Elgin, IL.
Poem by Alex Beale and Kevin Shergold quotation,
p.83, from *Little Fat Buzz*, compiled and edited by Chris Spencer, reprinted
by permission of Hodder and Stoughton Limited
'Faith is . . .' quotation, p.82, by David Forden, Palm Tree Press

Illustrations
Lynne Farmer, pp.18–19
Sue Fry, pp.10, 14–15, 17, 25, 27, 41, 43, 47, 61,
69, 77, 82, 85, 87

Photographs
Ken Bray, p.29 (below) and subsequent 'hands'
Daily Telegraph Colour Library © Mike Berkofsky, p.55
Lion Publishing/Jennie Karrach, pp.10–11, 37, 46–47,
68–69, 82–83, 91 ('snapshot' © Tony Stone);
/Brooke Snell, p.9; /Jon Willcocks, pp.92–93
Mick Rock, pp.29, 35, 39, 51, 57, 67, 73, 81, 89: many
thanks to Gillian and Chris
Pictorial Press, p.31
Spectrum, endpapers, p.22
John Williams Studios, Thame, pp.20–21
ZEFA, pp.13, 32, 36, 45, 49, 53, 59, 62–63, 65, 71, 75, 79

British Library Cataloguing in Publication Data
Stroud, Marion
    Just for you.
    1. Girls—Life skills guides
    2. Social skills
    I. Title
302'.02055   HQ798
ISBN 0 85648 910 7

Printed in Italy

Choices

You are someone special.
Whether your ambition is to turn the world
upside down, or to stay safely hidden
in the back row of life,
statistics show that you being 'you'
will have a noticeable effect on the lives
of at least 162 other people.
Your life *will* leave its mark.
In that you have no choice.
But you *can* begin to choose — *now* —
what kind of mark it will be.
For the choices you make today
will shape that future 'you',
who will share tears or laughter,
disappointment or satisfaction,
failure or success
with the world around you.

One day at a time

Resolutions
are things that we make on a birthday, on January 1
at the beginning of term, or on some other special occasion
and break five, six or seven days later.
Or, if we are feeling particularly strong,
they might linger on
for a month or two.
But this year
I am going to take one day at a time;
make my resolutions
for one day at a time.
Every day
I will try to do one thing
until it becomes a habit.
They say
that an action repeated every day
for three weeks
becomes a habit.
So throughout this year
I can develop these good habits
one day at a time
(with a few days off,
to give my will-power time to recover).

Just for today
I will concentrate on one of these:
☐ Be happy and smile, instead of scowling,
   at breakfast
☐ Eat sensibly and take some exercise,
   even if it's raining
☐ Get my homework done on time

☐ Tidy my room up *before* I'm asked
☐ Be patient with my little brother
   and stop arguing with my sister
☐ Pray when it isn't an emergency
☐ Finish the jumper I've been knitting for two years
☐ Write my diary *every* day
☐ Notice when Mum looks tired
☐ Spend five minutes doing something for someone else
☐ Remember that boys are people too and treat them kindly!
☐ Read the Bible for myself,
   so that I can find out what it really has to say
   about God and life and me

9

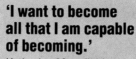

**'I want to become
all that I am capable
of becoming.'**
Katherine Mansfield

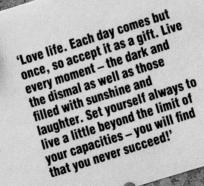

'Love life. Each day comes but
once, so accept it as a gift. Live
every moment – the dark and
the dismal as well as those
filled with sunshine and
laughter. Set yourself always to
live a little beyond the limit of
your capacities – you will find
that you never succeed!'

If you talk to me . . .

If you talk to me of God
please offer me more than a rule-book,
theories and ideas,
vague promises of greater understanding. . .
later on.
I need someone who has meaning
in my 'here and now'.

If you talk to me of God's Holy Spirit
please offer me more than a hovering dove,
beautifully pictured in stained glass.
Stained glass has not much
day-to-day usefulness.

If you talk to me of Jesus
please offer me more than a new-born
in a manger;
a gentle, bearded hippy
with a considerable fondness for children,
or a teller-of-tales
with a great capacity for being
misunderstood.

**What I need is a plan of life that has
meaning beyond the four walls of a
building; love that will never let me
down, and a leader I can follow with
confidence to the ends of the earth.**

If you talk to me of *that* God
then I will listen.

Just a mis-fit?

Dear Aunt Agony,

My parents came to this country before I was born, so I've always lived here. When I was small I was quite happy. But now, even though I've still got lots of friends, I feel as if I don't fit in. I'd like to go back and live with my grandparents; the stories I hear from my parents makes life there sound great. But I haven't got any money for the fare and Mum doesn't want me to go, so she won't help. Please advise me.

Yours,

Mis-fit

Dear Mis-fit,
I have news for you. Most of your friends feel just like you do at times, even if their families have lived in your town for generations. Of course, it is more difficult if your skin is a different colour, or your background and customs are not the same as other people's. But we all get that mis-fit feeling sometimes, especially when our looks, abilities, clothes or opportunities make us stand out from the crowd.

Don't think that living in another town or country will solve all your problems. Wherever you go, you take your biggest problem with you – because you can't get away from yourself! But a holiday visit to your grandparents sounds like a good idea. So, why not look for a Saturday job and start saving? It will give you something to look forward to and a chance to decide for yourself where you want to belong.

Bon voyage,
Your Agony Aunt

I look a freak

Dear Aunt Agony,

I've just had to have a brace put on my teeth. I look terrible: like a robot, all shiny metal. I daren't smile and everyone I meet makes jokes about it. It feels awful too. They say I've got to wear it for at least a year. I just can't stand it. My friend kept hers on for six weeks. Then she gave up. She says, 'Why worry about what you look like later on? It's now that counts. Get it taken off.' What do you think?

Yours,

Metal Mickey

Dear Metal Mickey,
I think your friend is so short-sighted that she probably needs glasses, as well as a brace on her teeth. OK, so you're uncomfortable now, but that will pass. So will the jokes – especially if you don't let them ruffle you. Just grin back. Remember that when you laugh, the world laughs with you. If you can relax and forget about it, others will do the same. Cheer up! It's the person you are that people relate to, not your teeth. In a year or two you'll be more than thankful that you stuck it out. On the bad days, imagine being famous and facing the TV cameras with crooked teeth. Or think about your wedding day smile, and stay with it.

Your Agony Aunt

Sometimes
I feel guilty . . .

Sometimes I feel guilty
about having so much to eat,
spending money on junk food
for snacks between meals
which I don't really need
but that become an enjoyable habit.

Sometimes I feel sad
when I see all those starving people
who gaze out at us
during the television news,
in between advertisements
for sausages and slimming mags.

Sometimes I feel angry,
because so many of us have too much
while others have too little.
And I talk about what I would do
if I were powerful and in control
of grain and butter mountains.

But sometimes I stop and think
that if everyone did something,
even if it were very little,
it would amount to a lot
in the end.

My Valentine

If I were St Valentine, I think that I would like to have my name linked with hearts and flowers and the beginning of love. I would be glad to be responsible for a day that comes just in time to brighten up that flat grey patch between New Year resolutions and Easter Eggs – even if it isn't a very dignified way of being remembered when you've died for your faith.

Dull school days sparkle as we discuss who is going to get what from whom, and what we shall do when it happens. Boring lessons go by in a dream as I imagine my secret admirer – tall, incredibly good-looking with a riveting personality – and totally fascinated by me! Then I feel like a freshly-poured glass of Coke, bubbly, desirable and darkly mysterious.

But there are other times when I feel like the dregs in the bottle; flat and left-over. I know, really, that there is no superman waiting in the wings to woo me. And if I insist on my dream-lover, I could just be this year's unclaimed Valentine – driven to sending a card to myself. So today I'll dream about meeting a real person I can care about; who is fun to be with, and who needs my friendship as much as I need his. Even if he has two left feet, a few spots, embarrassing relations, impatient friends, bad days and gloriously good days – just like me.

Second-hand blues

There's such a lot that's second-hand
in our house.

Second-hand car, second-hand furniture
— so 'sensible' and 'economical' for a growing
family! — second-hand books (Dad calls those
'collector's items') and second-hand clothes
— mostly worn by me.

And then there are all those 'family traditions' – the things we do at Christmas and at other times because Mum and Dad used to do them, way back.

I suppose it's good to have some things handed-on, accepting them because they've stood the test of time. They give us roots, a feeling of belonging.

But there's one thing that has to be firsthand for all of us
and that's what we believe.

This week my sister believes in reincarnation.

If that is true, I think it's highly likely that she will live her next life as a mule.

My brother spends his time looking for UFOs.

But I don't think we're going to be taken over by little green men in space suits.

Dad says that if we all worked harder the world would be a better place.

And Grandpa and Mum believe in God and faith and love and each life being special and for a purpose.

I think that I would like to be like them, peaceful and sure.

Perhaps I'll go their way.

But I still have to do it for myself,
think it through
test it out
and make my own decision.

Part-time job

Dear Aunt Agony,

I've got a part-time job. It's in a very trendy boutique and I'm lucky to have it, even if it's a bit boring at times. They let me buy things at a special price. And as I don't get much pocket money, the pay makes all the difference. The trouble is, I'm too tired when I get home to do my homework properly and I've got important exams coming up. Dad wants me to give up the job. He wants me to try for college. But I'm not sure! It would be so much easier to forget about exams. And I could always work at the boutique full-time, as soon as I'm old enough. What do you think?

Yours,

Good-time Girl

Dear Good-time Girl,
Stop and think. If the job is boring part-time, what would it be like five days a week, forty-nine weeks of the year? How does the money you're earning now compare with what you could expect from an interesting career, once you've got the necessary qualifications? Every job has its boring patches, but this one sounds as if it could be a dead-ender. You've got a lot of living ahead of you. I think it's time to take the long-term view.

    Studiously,
      Your Agony Aunt

25

Danger run

Dear Aunt Agony,

I have only been at this school for a few
months, and I've found it hard to settle in.
I was just beginning to make friends when
this craze started in the lunch-hour. They
call it Danger run. One girl takes something
from a shop and passes it to a friend who's
waiting outside. <u>She</u> then has to put it back
without being caught. Nearly all the girls
who are fun to be with are involved. They've
dared me to join in. If I don't, they say
they'll tell everyone I'm chicken. You can't
call it stealing, can you? But all the same,
I'm scared. What will happen if I do join in?
And what will happen if I don't? Please help.

   Yours,

      Chicken

Dear Chicken,
Keep out of it. Crazes don't usually last long and, if this one does, your class-mates won't have time to carry out their threats: they'll be far too busy dealing with furious shop-keepers, teachers and the police. Find something else to keep you busy in the lunch-hour – and tell them you haven't time to go into town. I know it's tough, but it will pass. Better to be a chicken than a goose.

Your Agony Aunt

Chas. Porter's band gave a concert at the Youth club tonight. 'Age of Fire', they call themselves... They certainly set <u>our</u> place alight! Being Chas's sister, Jenny was allowed to take the coffee 'backstage' in the interval — with my help. Steve Simmons, the drummer, chatted to me for ages. He's =REALLY= nice! I thought he might be a bit 'big-headed'. The band is getting lots of bookings. Steve's in the year ahead of me at school — can't think why I haven't noticed him before. THIS makes Monday morning seem a lot more interesting!!! — Glad I was wearing my new jeans!

Crying for a dream

Last summer Mary fell in love – with Ziggy Zullerman, lead guitarist of the League of Gold. For nine long months she talked about him, dreamed about him, wrote *to* him and read every word written *about* him. His face gazed down from every corner of her room, and she played his records so often that the cat rushed out into the garden as the first thunderous notes set her ornaments rattling on the shelf. Mary was a Ziggy Zullerman fan – until yesterday.

Yesterday Ziggy Zullerman died; collapsed in the street clutching a guitar case packed full of drugs. Ziggy could not play any more. Could not play, unless he shut the world out first. Shut out his fans, people like Mary whose adoration had once been a stepping-stone to success, but was now a terrible weight on his shoulders, crushing him . . . forcing him to try to do more and be more than any one human being can hope to be, alone.

Today Mary is crying. Crying for a dream that is broken in pieces. Crying for the person she thought she loved and who never really existed. Crying for the real Ziggy Zullerman . . . a lonely young man who appeared to have everything and really had nothing.

Just the age I am

There are times when I wish I was older
not so hemmed in
by rules and regulations.
There are times when I wish I was younger
so that I did not have to make
decisions about the future.
But at the moment I am glad to be
just the age I am
because I can still . . .
watch cartoons on TV,
stand on my head,
swing from the climbing-frame by my legs,
run barefoot through the park
and tell my secrets to the dog.
Or, if I like, I can spend . . .
an hour in the bathroom putting on my face,
a morning in my bedroom thinking about life,
a day in town trying on the latest fashions,
a warm star-lit evening, walking
hand-in-hand with you . . .
And nobody is a bit surprised!

STRICTLY PRIVATE

Two whole weeks, and I've seen 'Steve S.' twice! -Across the dining room last Friday lunch time, and today, coming out of the library. I must look pretty different in school clothes, because he glanced at me, half-smiled, looked again and then said "Hello"! WHY OH WHY did I have to go bright red and drop all my books?! Sally and Debbie were nudging me and giggling like a couple of hyenas. By the time I'd picked everything up, he'd gone!.. I don't suppose he'll ever speak to me again. Coming home, I wondered if I might just 'drop in' to see Jenny - when the band were at her house practising. But she said they've got to use a hut in the middle of a field now, because the neighbours complained.

Good friends

I'm glad that it's the custom
for girls to give each other birthday gifts,
(even if the boys make fun
of the time we spend choosing,
and the money we spend buying)
because it gives me the chance to tell you
that a friend like you is really good news.

You always seem to have
the right thing to say,
and find the right moment to say it.
When you are here
laughter comes more easily,
hurts are soothed more rapidly,
problems seem smaller
and good days are better.
There are, of course, times
when we argue — hurt one another's feelings.
But then I know
that I can always come to you and say
'I'm sorry' — and you'll be waiting,
or maybe ringing on my bell
to say it first.
A friend like you is a gift no money could buy.
So thank you for being my friend.

IT'S HAPPENED! Steve has asked me out! Well, not "out" exactly, but he walked me home from the shops. (I'll never grumble about running errands for mum again!) _And_ we talked for ten minutes at the gate.. _And_ he asked if I'd be watching the match tomorrow. I wasn't going, but I'll be there now! (didn't tell _him_ that, of course!) Can this be love? I feel like dancing round the room, shouting and singing... anything but doing homework on a night like this.

Too fat

Dear Aunt Agony,

My friend and I are definitely overweight. Tina's Mum says that 'being big' runs in their family. Mine says that it's 'puppy fat' and we'll grow out of it. We want to be slim now. But when we cut out school dinners we get so hungry we have to buy a bar of chocolate after school to keep us going till we get home. Can you help?

Yours,

Rumbletum

Dear Rumbletum,
Missing meals isn't the way to get slim and stay healthy. You need to apply a bit of science.

BE DEFINITE. If you don't know what you should weigh (and that depends on your own height and build) check up and make that your goal. Look in your local bookshop or the library for good diet books with ideal weight charts.

BE SENSIBLE. Eating nothing but grapefruit for a week will make you lose weight. It will also make you ill. Choose a balanced diet that includes plenty of fresh fruit and vegetables, food that is high in natural fibre and low in fat and sugar.

BE PATIENT. You didn't get overweight in a day and you won't lose it all immediately either. Two pounds a week is a realistic target and will soon show a difference.

BE ACTIVE. Walking, cycling, keep-fit, swimming, jogging or dancing all help to burn up calories and keep your mind off food.

BE DETERMINED. But there's more to life than a size 10 figure so

DON'T BE A DIET BORE.
Excuse me while I hop on the scales.

Your Agony Aunt

Wanted — a boyfriend

Dear Aunt Agony,

Sharon's the only one in our gang who's never had a boyfriend. She thinks it's because she's too tall and her Mum won't let her spend much on clothes — says she's still growing too fast. But I'm not sure it's really that. She hasn't any brothers and she doesn't seem to know what to say to the boys we meet, especially when they tease her. But she's desperate to find someone, anyone! I think it's so that she's got a boy-friend to discuss, like the rest of us. How can we help?

Yours,

Paired-off

Dear Paired-off,
How about broadening the range of your conversation? There *are* other things in this world worthy of your attention, you know. So try talking about them more often when Sharon is around. It's natural to want friends of the opposite sex – but they should be friends first, and 'boys' second, or the friendship will soon fizzle out. And why not offer Sharon the loan of a scarf or belt or jewellery that would give her outfit a lift? If you *all* exchange ideas and experiment with each other's things, she won't feel the odd one out. Encourage her to develop her own good points and be a person in her own right – and one day her prince will come.

Your Agony Aunt

43

Bottom of the class

I came bottom in that test again today, God.
I know someone has to be bottom,
but why does it always have to be me?
If I was teacher's pet
like some people I know, but won't mention,
I might do better.
On the other hand
I suppose that if I did my homework,
learned the stuff properly, before the last minute,
it would make all the difference.

But you know how it is with school.
Once you fail a few times,
no one expects you
to do very much.
And then it's tempting
to take the soft option,
go out with your friends, watch TV,
play your records, anything rather than think about
subjects which seem so utterly pointless
in everyday life.

Well, I'll try again, God, if you'll help me.
Help me to listen in class, remember my books,
stop playing the fool — even if that's what everyone
expects of me now.
I know I can't be good at everything.
But maybe I could be good at something,
if you would help me.
Please, God?

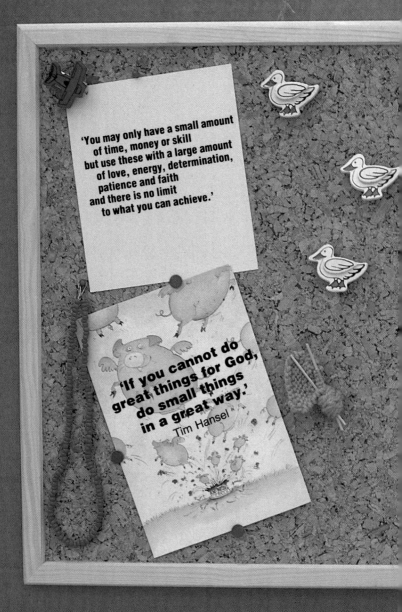

'You may only have a small amount
of time, money or skill
but use these with a large amount
of love, energy, determination,
patience and faith
and there is no limit
to what you can achieve.'

'If you cannot do
great things for God,
do small things
in a great way.'
Tim Hansel

Decisions, decisions

A centipede was happy till
One day, a toad in fun
Said 'Pray, which leg goes after which?'
Which strained his mind to such a pitch
He lay distracted in a ditch
Considering how to run!

Sometimes I think that life would be easier
if I did not have to make so many decisions –
if no one asked me
    which subjects I intended to study next term
    where I wanted to go on holiday next year
    what I wanted to do when I left school.

Sometimes I seem to be so busy
    planning for the future
    or solving problems from the past
that I don't have any time
    for living at this moment
    that I have now.

Please God
    help me to know
        how much my yesterdays and tomorrows
    should be allowed to colour
        my today.

STRICTLY PRIVATE

It's official! We're going out!!! Steve asked me last night if I'd like to go roller skating with him and the rest of the band on Wednesday. Not exactly my dream of a candle-lit supper for two in that little Italian place near the station... but pocket money and a paper round don't stretch to luxuries! - Anyway, Mum and Dad have said we have to do our "going out" in a crowd. Why do _I_ have to have such fussy parents? They're not just old-fashioned - they're _museum_ pieces! Anyone would think they didn't trust me. What's _worse_, they want Steve to come to tea on _Sunday_, so they can meet him.... and Aunty Bea will be here.... she's bound to wheeze all over him and suck her false teeth. I wonder if Suzy would lend me her roller boots for a bit of practice? Otherwise I shall probably fall flat on my face on Wednesday, and _die_ of shame!

LOVE IS

Steve & me!

Just an ordinary day

Today I exercised the dog, cycled to school, walked into town, telephoned a friend.

Today was just an ordinary day.

Today I had a long and unexpected letter from a cousin far away, found the dress I had wanted for weeks reduced to just the price I could afford, and got good marks for a test I was sure I had failed. Dad said nice things about my cooking, and I discussed a problem with Mum without losing my temper.

Today I watched the sunset, said sorry to Sarah – and felt rotten about the way I had treated everybody yesterday . . . until I remembered. Remembered that when God forgives, he forgets – which means that I can, too.

Then I felt suddenly glad, and sang in the bath.

So today was just an ordinary day . . . or was it?

Against the stream

Why should doing the right thing so often seem
far less rewarding
than doing the wrong?
You would think
that obeying that niggling little voice inside
should earn you a pat on the back,
instead of taunts and laughter from your friends,
most of whom seem to be having far more fun
going *with* the stream
than you do, swimming against it.

It's hard, standing up for what you believe in,
being different,
at times opting out of the 'in crowd'.
Sometimes, it is too hard
and then you give in, and 'live a little'.
But that kind of living leaves a nasty taste
in the cold light of day.
And you realize
that it's not just your friends
to whom you must answer —
it's yourself.

STRICTLY PRIVATE

We've had a <u>ROW</u>!!! - Not just a little disagreement (we often have those) but a RED-HOT, SIZZLING, ROW! - when we both shouted - and accused each other of awful things. Liz Martin invited us to her Farewell Party (her dad is going to work abroad). But Steve said he couldn't make it...'because of the band'. He said the most important booking they'd had so far was on the next evening, and Chas. had written a lot of new songs for it, so they <u>must</u> practise. I would have thought that one night wouldn't have made much difference - if he'd really <u>wanted</u> to come. But he doesn't like barn dances (even if I do!) and he's not too keen on Liz (even if she <u>is</u> one of my best friends) - so the band is a good excuse. He seems to think that what he likes and wants to do is all that matters: <u>I</u> should just 'fall into line.' - Well, he can think again! I shall go to the party by myself.

The most fantastic boy

Dear Aunt Agony,

I've been asked out by this fantastic boy. He's in the school tennis team, good-looking, popular....all my friends think I'm very lucky. There's just one snag. I'm a Christian but he doesn't believe in God and teases me about my beliefs. He's asked me to partner him in a tournament on Sunday. I said I usually went to church. But he just grinned and said he could show me better ways of spending my time. I don't know what to do. I like him so much. Maybe, I could persuade him to believe, if I really got to know him. Mum says that I'm much more likely to go his way, but I don't see why I should. After all, Christians are supposed to tell other people about God, aren't they? Who do you think is right?

Yours,

Uncertain

Dear Uncertain,
I think you're both right!
Christians are certainly
intended to have friends who
believe and friends who don't –
as Jesus himself did. But if you
are a Christian and your
boyfriend is determined in his
belief that God does not exist,
you've got no foundation on
which to build a lasting
relationship. Deep friendship is
born out of shared interests –
and what we believe influences
our attitudes in every area of
life. To begin a relationship
intending to change the other
person (which, it seems, you
both want to do!) is a quick
route to a lot of unhappiness.
Be good friends, by all means,
but keep the 'going-out'
relationship for someone with
whom you can really share
things at every level. That's
well worth waiting for.

Your Agony Aunt

Trouble getting up

Dear Aunt Agony,

I have trouble getting up in the mornings; I don't seem able to move my legs. My mother thinks it's laziness - she doesn't understand how hard I work. Should I see a doctor?

Yours,

Weak-at-the-Knees

Are you listening, God?

I've got to talk to somebody, God. Are you listening?
I suppose you're the best person to confide in
because you made me in the first place.
But I can't help wondering at times whether
you made a mistake – now and then, here and there.

It's me I'm having trouble with, God
(and my brother and my sister and my parents
and my boyfriend),
but mostly me . . . and my feelings.
I can't understand
why I nearly burst with the sheer joy of living one day,
and then go tumbling down into the depths of despair
the next.
Sometimes it isn't even one mood a day, it's several.
And I don't like me then, any more than my family does.
Mum says it's all part of growing up.
But if that's true, why doesn't everyone else feel this way?

Jenny is so quick with the funny answer
– she never misses the point of the joke.
Mary is so calm, never argumentative or rebellious.
And Liz doesn't make mistakes in front of the whole class
like I do.
Can they really be as uncertain and up-and-downish
as I am, inside?
Is it true that we are all in this together?
If it is, God, please help me not to wallow in my misery
or hug my problems to myself,
but to accept the help that others want to give.
And please keep me from being so occupied with myself
that I don't notice when others are hurting.

Do's and Don'ts

Please don't tell me how wrong I was
because I know, and feel sorry for doing it,
but telling me makes it harder.
to apologize.

Please don't tell me how lucky I am
because I know and feel guilty for grumbling,
but telling me makes it harder
to be thankful.

Please don't tell me how foolish I've been
because I know, and feel ashamed of the mess I've made,
but telling me makes it harder
to ask for help.

But please *do* tell me that you love me,
because, although you think I know, I sometimes doubt it,
and telling me again makes it easier
to want to be different.

STRICTLY PRIVATE

This has been the most miserable week of my entire life. I couldn't sleep (until it was time to get up) - so I was late for school three times. I couldn't eat, but I didn't lose any weight. There was no Steve, no phone calls, no letters - and the television broke down. School was awful. Even the weather joined in : one grey dreary day after another. But tonight the sky is blazing with red and gold. The lights in my life have all been switched on again too, because we've <u>made it up!</u> I never thought it would be so hard - or take so long - to say 'I'm sorry'. Only two little words, but they stick in your throat like a lump of lead. I wrote a letter in the end - but it was still in the post when Steve came round. So we've made it up. But I wish it hadn't happened : Those awful angry words have left a mark on something that was beautiful.

S.W.A.L.K.

LOVE !
LOVE !
LOVE !

Last night I met a problem
So I stormed and stamped and shouted;
And when that problem faced me still
I whined and wept and pouted!
Today I tried another tack,
I faced it with a grin.
I haven't solved that problem yet
But I know who's going to win!

Faith is knowing that when God allows problems they are really opportunities in disguise.

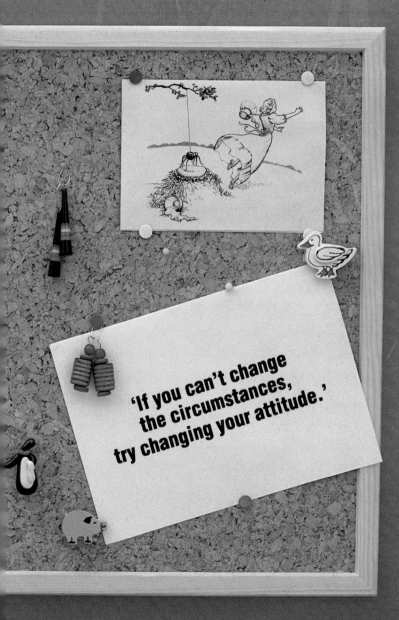

'If you can't change
the circumstances,
try changing your attitude.'

Someone special

I've always found it hard to imagine
how my life could have any particular significance
in the general scheme of things.
For when I compare myself with other people,
I'm so depressingly average,
without anything – that's not embarrassing –
to make me stand out from the crowd.
In fact I have quite often felt
like that girl Lara in the Russian novel
who, when dead, became
'A nameless number, on a list that was later mislaid.'
But today all that has changed,
because today I have discovered
that God loves us as we are
without waiting until we do great things
and become someone that everyone wants to know.
But though he loves us as we are,
he doesn't leave us as we are.
Instead he teaches and trains us
so that we are equipped
to do the things that he has specially planned
for us to do.
Which, if I can find the way he works it out in practice,
will make my life quite an adventure.

STRICTLY PRIVATE

I don't think rock bands are all they're cracked up to be. I used to imagine that going to the concerts _with_ the band would be fantastic, but not any more! I'm tired of holding leads, switching lights on and off, and being deafened when they test the sound levels. To say nothing of being shouted at for standing in the wrong place, or sitting on someone's music. No wonder Jenny doesn't come early to help very often. I'm beginning to wonder if Steve would notice if I wasn't around - though he _says_ I'm a 'great help' and he _really_ wants me to be there. What _I_ really want is to be with him, to know that he is thinking about us, for a change.

Mum says, 'spend time with your other friends.' Develop interests of your own. Don't try to live in Steve's pocket. Be your own person.' She must have forgotten what it's like to be in love. The trouble is, I'm pretty sure that _I_ love Steve ... but I'm not sure that he really loves me.

Ups and downs

Dear Aunt Agony,

I've just come back from the Youth Group holiday. It was great. You should have seen those mountains we climbed. The sun shone every day. We had a laugh a minute. And it seemed so easy to believe in God – there. Now we're home. My sister borrowed my clothes again; the preacher this morning was boring, and it's raining. Why don't good feelings last?

Yours,

Fed-up

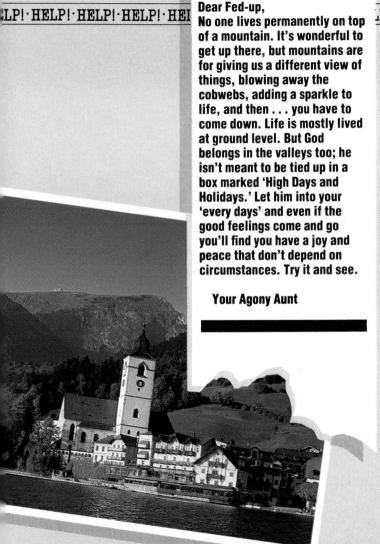

Dear Fed-up,
No one lives permanently on top of a mountain. It's wonderful to get up there, but mountains are for giving us a different view of things, blowing away the cobwebs, adding a sparkle to life, and then . . . you have to come down. Life is mostly lived at ground level. But God belongs in the valleys too; he isn't meant to be tied up in a box marked 'High Days and Holidays.' Let him into your 'every days' and even if the good feelings come and go you'll find you have a joy and peace that don't depend on circumstances. Try it and see.

Your Agony Aunt

Changing church

Dear Aunt Agony,

My parents go to a church that I find
very boring.   There's hardly anyone
there under thirty-five. I want to go
to my best friend's church, which is
really great and quite near to where
I live. I go to their Youth Club,
because at our church there isn't any
youth! But Mum and Dad grumble if I
ask to go there on Sundays. It's not
'our' denomination and they do
things differently there. I don't
want to hurt their feelings, but we
often end up having rows about it.
How can I persuade them to see
things my way?

　　Yours,

　　Modern Millie

Dear Millie,
Stand back for a minute and ask yourself *why* you want to change churches. Is it to enjoy yourself with your friends? Or do you really find it easier to worship and learn more about God there? Ask God to help you sort your motives out. If you are convinced you want to change for the right reasons, but your parents are still uneasy, see if they would accept a compromise. If you go *willingly* and *cheerfully* to their church on a Sunday morning, perhaps they would allow you to go with your friends in the evening. You could suggest they join you for a service there, to see for themselves what it's like. Whatever happens, try to go to church prepared to give as well as to get – and you will be surprised how different things will seem.

Your Agony Aunt

Times I get scared

**'If thou hast a fearful thought, share it
not with a weakling; whisper it to thy
saddle-bow and ride forth singing.'**

Someone stuck that quote on the class-
room wall. It was King Alfred who said it.
    It isn't '*if*' I have a fearful thought
really, though, it's more a case of '*when*'.
Because you know, God, that I do quite a
lot of worrying, on the quiet. I don't talk
about it much, but sometimes, in bed at
night, I think about things – awful things –
that could happen and do happen to some
people. There are people at school whose
parents or grandparents have had cancer,
or heart attacks, lost their jobs, got
divorced. It could happen in our family,
God, and if it did, what would I do?
    Then there are the great big nightmare
things – nuclear war, famines and
earthquakes – and people being put in
prison for what they believe. I don't think
my little bit of faith would stand up to
torture. I try very hard to trust you, God, to
believe that you are in control. But I can't
help wondering sometimes why you don't
stop it, if you are.
    Please help me, God. Help me to
know for sure that if any of these problems
do threaten me, I shan't face them alone.
That you really will give me the courage

and strength I need, right then, when I
need it.

It's good to put my worries into
words. Brought out into the open, they
seem much smaller. Thank you for
listening, God. I couldn't talk to my friends
like this. We would probably scare each
other silly. But thank you that I'm quite
safe in bringing all my fearful thoughts to
you.

STRICTLY PRIVATE

Steve says it's over. That he doesn't want to go out with me any more. There's no-one else; he wants to stay 'good friends', but he just doesn't want to be tied down at the moment. I don't understand it. What has made him go off me? Is it something I said?...or did... or didn't do? I pleaded with him to give it another try. Said that I would try to change; try to be the kind of girl he wants.... But I knew that wouldn't work, even as I said it, because I have got to be _me_. I can't act a part just to make someone like me more. That kind of loving doesn't last. And I don't want to be just good friends: I want to be special to HIM.. It hurts not to be wanted. What's even worse is that everyone else seems to have seen it coming for weeks. What's the matter with _me_? AM I BLIND OR SOMETHING?!

Please God, help me to get over it. Help me not to feel sick every time I hear his name, or one of the songs he played... And please, help me never to hurt anyone like he has hurt me.

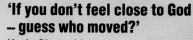

**'If you don't feel close to God
– guess who moved?'**
Kevin Shergold

'Please welcome this lump of dejection
That is me, Father
I can't lift up my head
I can't start to look for you
But please take me as I am
And help me through the dark.
I can't offer you energy
Or enthusiasm
I can't offer you love
Or worship
I can only offer me
Drawn in and hurting
Please hold me gently, Lord.'
Alex Beale

Parent problems

Dear Aunt Agony,

My friend has awful problems with her Mum. They just don't seem to understand each other at all. They're always rowing. Debbie says that her mother doesn't like her friends, her clothes, her records, or anything about her. She makes her stay in when she wants to go out, and Debbie has to go out to things when she would far rather stay at home. I'm afraid that one day she'll run away. If her mother is really as mean as Debbie says she is, someone ought to <u>do</u> something. What can I do to help?

Yours,

Friend-in-need

Dear Friend-in-need,
Don't take sides. There are two versions of every story. You are probably doing the best thing you can by being a listening ear. Don't feel that you must offer advice. Debbie needs to talk to someone she can trust not to repeat her confidences. But we all tend to exaggerate when we're mad with someone. Things may not be as black as she paints them. If the trouble continues, encourage her to confide in someone older. Teachers or youth leaders can be very understanding – yes, really – or your Mum might have a chat with Debbie's Mum – if they know each other. The most important thing is to be a peace-maker, not a trouble-maker. Stick with it.

Your Agony Aunt

Danger – keep off!

Dear Aunt Agony,

Some girls at school have been playing with a ouija board in the lunch hour. One or two things that it has told them have come true. Now it has told the girl who owns the board that she has only two years to live. She is having awful dreams and is scared stiff, although most of the others are trying to laugh it off. Please help.

Yours,

Very Worried

86

Dear Very Worried,
Ouija boards are not toys. Those girls have been playing with fire. There are real spiritual forces at work in our world – both good and evil. Our physical senses may not recognize them, but that doesn't alter the fact. Ouija boards, automatic writing, seances and the like work through contact with those evil spiritual forces. Many people don't realize what they are getting involved with. All contact with the occult is out (the Bible actually says that God forbids it for his people); this is for our own mental and spiritual good. The girls who have been fooling around with the ouija board should get rid of it straight away. For their own good, they should make up their minds to have nothing to do with such things in future. They can also pray, asking God's forgiveness for getting involved with something he forbids, even if they did so quite innocently, and ask his help to take away their fears. If your friend's problems persist, persuade her to talk to a responsible older person in your church and ask them to pray with her.

I'm glad you're taking this seriously.

Your Agony Aunt

STRICTLY PRIVATE

I've done it! I've seen Steve and spoken to him without bursting into tears or saying something stupid. And it wasn't anything like as hard as I expected it to be. Thinking about it was far worse than the actual event.. but I'm glad I've done it. I can't spend the rest of my life walking the long way home rather than passing his house, or keeping away from the Youth Club in case he comes in. Suddenly I feel <u>free</u>! In a funny kind of way, I'm enjoying it! It's good to have time to look in the shops with Jenny. It's nice to please <u>myself</u> what I wear, without wondering if he will like it ...If this is Women's Lib, I think I might be in favour. I shall concentrate on my work, prepare to be a career woman — for this term at least!

Thankyou letter

Dear Family,

At school we were talking about giving. Our teacher said that giving was one of the most important, the most difficult and the most neglected gifts of all. For homework she told us to write down at least one thing that we could thank each of our family for. Just for once, I shan't mind if you read this over my shoulder.

MUM AND DAD: Thank you for caring enough to say 'no' sometimes – even when I argue. I feel safer knowing that I'm not the one who has to put the limits on my freedom. Thank you for knowing when I need to talk, and for having the patience to let me test my ideas out on you – for not (usually) saying 'Don't be silly' or 'It can't be done' and often suggesting, 'Let's try.'

SUZY: I'm glad I've got a sister like you to borrow clothes from, confide in, shout at, and gang up with against the world.

TOM: You're very good value when it comes to keeping silence and boredom at bay!

GRAN AND GRANDPA: Thank you for being unshockable and unshakeably on my side. With you I have learned about knitting, playing hopscotch, changing a fuse, fishing with maggots – and about God. I know I can always count on you.

Today I realize that I'm very lucky to belong to this family.
Thank you all for being you.

Presents

'If there is not enough darkness in all the world to put out the light of one small candle of compassion it is better by far to light that candle than to curse the darkness.'

'Small gleams of caring become an arc-light of love.'

'You give but little
when you give of your possessions.
It is when you give of yourself
that you truly give.'

'God loved the world so much
that he gave his only Son so
that everyone who believes in
him may not die but have
eternal life. For God did not
send his Son into the world to
be its judge, but to be its
Saviour.'
The Bible: Gospel of John,
chapter three

What can I give Him
Poor as I am
If I were a shepherd, I would bring a lamb
If I were a wise man I would play my part
What I can I give Him – give my heart.
Christina Rossetti